Only In Dreams:

A Book of Quotes

Only In Dreams:

A Book of Quotes

Edited by Simon Pettet

BARNES
&NOBLE
BOOKS
NEW YORK

Compilation copyright © 2003 by Barnes & Noble, Inc.

2003 Barnes & Noble Books

ISBN 0-7607-4060-7

Printed and bound in the United States of America

M 9 8 7 6 5 4 3 2 1

WE ALL DREAM, EVEN THOSE OF US WHO DON'T remember our dreams. The sublime fact of what psychologist Carl Jung so aptly named "the collective unconscious"—the shared pool, the communion of dreams—is here celebrated in a gathering of two hundred pithy and provocative observations on dreams, dreaming, and the dream state.

Writers and thinkers in all cultures throughout history have recognized this special state—source of our constructive, unifying, creative, poetic faculties; source of our "true" selves: the unconscious mind, potential source of prophecy and wisdom. How extraordinary that each of us spends so many hours of our lives asleep! How strange we still have so little idea as to the true nature of those mysterious hours. Or do we?

We have long pondered the significance of our dreams. Are they mere froth that the mind churns up, quirky minutiae of the day-to-day, as some still argue? Or are they (they must surely be) something more fundamental, more profound—divine promptings?—

or, at any rate, deeply buried, deeply ingrained *self*-promptings, *soul*-promptings?, Keys, secrets, road maps?

Long before Sigmund Freud, in second-century Greece the oneirologist [sic] Artimedorus sought an interpretative framework. *He who dreams of a snake . . . He who dreams of gold . . . He who dreams of a terrible calamity . . .* Such simpleminded equations remain eternally popular. There is a thirst. We genuinely want to know. To use Jungian terms again, we wish to integrate this uncharted dream life into the totality of our consciousness.

But first, we need to recognize that this "other world" is our consciousness, ultimately indistinguishable from the more familiar, but no less dreamlike, waking state. Chuang Tse's hauntingly familiar paradox echoes through the ages here: was I a man dreaming I was a butterfly? or a butterfly dreaming I was a man? Or, to take its counterpoint from Kafka: am I a man or an insect? I think I am, I fear I am, I dream myself—can actually *experience* myself, vividly—as some loathsome bug.

Dreams, it scarcely needs to be pointed out, may be heavenly visions; they might also be Nightmares. The bulk of dreams in this collection are visions of hope. Dreams remind us. We have limitless imaginative resources. We can indeed dream what we fear; we can also dream what we want.

Dreams, then, as a metaphor for aspiration (and inspiration), avoiding, if possible, cliché and sentiment or else transforming that cliché and sentiment, as in some of the pop lyrics cited here, into surprising profundity. Life *is* but a dream—sh-boom! We *do* search for our "dream lover." Dreams *are* our nightly refuge, our private strength.

The heterogeneity, multiplicity, and variety of observations presented here (from mystics and politicians to movie stars and stand-up comedians—not to mention psychologists, psychiatrists, neurologists, neuroscientists) is, of course, entirely intentional. Dreams, multi-faceted phenomena, demand a multi-faceted approach.

Even the fragmentary quality, the quotation form, is fitting. Dreams are, by their very nature, partial. We catch only a glimpse in the dream state. We get an inkling. But the whole is not vouchsafed to us. Then we wake up!

One is reminded of recent developments in dream research: the extraordinary breakthrough of REM (rapid eye movement) analysis; the thrilling concept of so-called lucid dreaming (waking in the dream to an awareness that you are dreaming); possible insights available through positron emission tomography (PET) scans, which allow us to examine the brain when dreaming in ways we have never before been able. Our understanding grows more sophisticated. At the same time, it is the primitive nature of the dream that persists. We may examine the dreamer, but the dream remains forever elusive. For all the reams and reams of analysis, there is still only you—creator, director, choreographer, "star," of your own personal "inner movie." You—would you wish to have it any other way?—are master or mistress of all possibilities, master or mistress of your own fate.

—*Simon Pettet*

Only
In Dreams

Dreams that have wings
And dreams that have honey, and dreams that
    have stings
Dreams of the maker, and dreams of the teller,
Dreams of the kitchen, and dreams of the cellar.

—BEN JONSON

O what land is the Land of Dreams? What are its
mountains and what are its streams?

—WILLIAM BLAKE

Once traced in faint and visionary colours, like
writings in sympathetic ink, they were drawn out,
by the fierce chemistry of my dreams, into insuf-
ferable splendour that fretted my heart.

—THOMAS DE QUINCEY

A dream is nothing else but a bubbling scum
Or froth of the fancy, which the day hath
Left undigested, or the after-feast made of
The fragments of idle imagination.

—THOMAS NASHE

I hold that it is true that dreams are faithful
    interpreters of our drives,
but there is an art to sorting and understanding
    them.

—MICHEL DE MONTAIGNE

When good dreams fall, I do with joy pursue them
When bad ones fall, I pray I may eschew them.

—ARTIMEDORUS

Father, O father! What do we here
In this land of unbelief and fear?
The Land of Dreams is better far
Above the light of the morning star.

—WILLIAM BLAKE

Last night as I was sleeping
I dreamt—marvelous error!
that there was a fiery sun here in my heart.

—ANTONIO MACHADO

Dreams do come true, if we only wish hard enough.
You can have anything in life if you will sacrifice
everything else for it.

—JAMES M. BARRIE

I have done no other thing by day and night but meditate and spend my spirit in the judgment of dreams.

—ARTIMEDORUS

Ground not upon dreams; you know they are ever contrary.

—THOMAS MIDDLETON

Hold fast to dreams
For if dreams die
Life is a broken-winged bird
That can't fly.

—LANGSTON HUGHES

Tell me not, in mournful numbers,
"Life is but an empty dream!"
For the soul is dead that slumbers,
And things are not what they seem.

—HENRY WADSWORTH LONGFELLOW

Reality is wrong. Dreams are for real.

—TUPAC SHAKUR

True, I talk of dreams
Which are the children of an idle brain
Begot of nothing but vain fantasy...

—WILLIAM SHAKESPEARE

In dreams we produce the picture
which will arouse the emotions we need for
    our purpose,
that is, for solving problems confronting us at
    the time of the dream
in accordance with a particular style of life
    which is ours.

—ALFRED ADLER

The point, as Marx saw it, is that dreams never come true.

—HANNAH ARENDT

If dreams were understood, they would lose their purpose.

—ALFRED ADLER

Dreams and visions are infused into man for their advantage and instruction.

—Artimedorus

Peace can be reached through meditation on the knowledge which dreams give.

—Patanjali

The action of the imaginative faculty during sleep is the same as at the time when it receives a prophecy.

—Moses Maimonides

An uninterpreted dream is like an unread letter.

—Rabbi Hisda

When we can't dream any longer we die.

—EMMA GOLDMAN

Writing is nothing more than a guided dream.

—JORGE LUIS BORGES

Thinking is the mind's labor, dreaming its pleasure.

—VICTOR HUGO

The more one is concerned with solution of dreams, the more one is driven to recognize that the majority of the dreams of adults deal with sexual material and give expression to erotic wishes. A judgment on this point can be formed only by those who really analyze dreams.

—SIGMUND FREUD

All elongated objects, such as sticks, tree trunks and umbrellas…may stand for the male organ. Boxes, cases, chests, cupboards and ovens represent the uterus, and also hollow objects, ships, and vessels of all kinds.

—SIGMUND FREUD

To reap, to gather, or to prune vines, if one dreams of these activities out of season, it means delay in all affairs and undertakings until the proper time and season for that process.

—ARTIMEDORUS

Perhaps our dreaming consciousness is primarily concerned with the survival of the species and only secondarily with the individual.

—MONTAGUE ULLMAN, M.D.

A bunch of grapes, both in and out of season, is a good omen, since it generally signifies benefits received through or from women. White grapes presage open gains; black grapes, secret ones.

—ARTIMEDORUS

A skilful man reads his dreams for his self-knowledge; yet not the details but the quality. These whimsical pictures, in as much as they originate from us, may well have an analogy with our whole life and fate.

—RALPH WALDO EMERSON

A dreamer is one who can only find his way by moonlight, and his punishment is that he sees the dawn before the rest of the world.

—OSCAR WILDE

That which the dream shows is the shadow of such wisdom as exists in man, even during his waking state he may know nothing about it. We do not know it because we are fooling away our time with outward and perishing things, and are asleep in regard to that which is real within ourself.

—PARACELSUS

If one advances confidently in the direction
    of his dreams
and endeavors to live the life which he has
    imagined,
he will meet with success unexpected
    in common hours.

—HENRY DAVID THOREAU

The future belongs to those who believe in the beauty of their dreams.

—ELEANOR ROOSEVELT

Most people never run far enough on their first wind to find out they've got a second. Give your dreams all you've got and you'll be amazed at the energy that comes out of you.

—WILLIAM JAMES

To dream magnificently is not a gift given to all men, and even for those who possess it, it has a strong risk of being progressively diminished by the over-growing dissipation of modern life. The ability to dream is a divine and mysterious ability.

—CHARLES BAUDELAIRE

Every dream is a prophecy: every jest is an earnest in the womb of Time.

—GEORGE BERNARD SHAW

Dreams are important spontaneous products of the unconscious psyche, outside the control of will. They are pure nature; they show us the unvarnished, natural truth and are therefore fitted, as nothing else is, to give back an attitude that accords with our basic human nature when our consciousness has strayed too far from its foundations and run into an impasse.

—CARL G. JUNG

Dream is not a revelation. If a dream affords the dreamer some light on himself, it is not the person with closed eyes who makes the discovery, but the person with open eyes lucid enough to fit thoughts together. Dream—a scintillating mirage surrounded by shadows—is essentially poetry.

—MICHEL LEIRIS

Dreams are true while they last, and do we not
live in dreams?

—ALFRED LORD TENNYSON

But you see, it is very difficult, for always there is
a dream dreaming us.

—KALAHARI (SOUTH AFRICA) BUSHMAN quoted in
Laurens Van Der Post, *The Heart of the Matter*

That we come to this earth to live is untrue
We come but to sleep, to dream.

—ANONYMOUS AZTEC POEM

To believe in one's dreams is to spend all of ones
life asleep.

—CHINESE PROVERB

He who loses his dreaming is lost.

It is true that there are dreams which embody suppressed wishes and fears, but what is there which the dream cannot on occasion embody?

—CARL G. JUNG

You ask me what it is I do when I dream? I will tell you what you do when you are awake. You take me, the rest of my dream, and the totality of your past and you force me, by making me smaller and smaller, to fit into the little circle that you trace around your present action.

—HENRI BERGSON

The dream is the theater where the dreamer is at once scene, actor, prompter, stage manager, author, audience, and critic.

—CARL G. JUNG

I dream in my dream the dreams of the other
    dreamers,
And I become the other dreamers.

—WALT WHITMAN

The interpretation of dreams is the *Via Regia* (the Royal Road) to the knowledge of the unconscious in mental life.

—SIGMUND FREUD

From the beginning, we must infer, man was a
     dreaming animal. . .
it was the dream that opened man's eyes to new
     possibilities in his waking life.

—Lewis Mumford

Myth is the public dream, and dream is the private
myth.

—Joseph Campbell

Both dreams and myths are important communi-
cations. If we do not understand the language in
which they are written, we miss a great deal of
what we know and tell ourselves in those hours
when we are not busy manipulating the outside
world.

—Erich Fromm

I am against nature. I think nature is very unnatural. I think the truly natural things are dreams, which nature can't touch with decay.

—BOB DYLAN

I dream, therefore I exist.

—AUGUST STRINDBURG

The literature of the subject contains various examples of the influence of one dreamer by another.

—WILHELM STEKEL

The dreaming process…seems to be incorporated in…(a) broader regulative mechanism.

—SAMUEL LOWY

Dreams are not to be likened to the unregulated sounds that rise from a musical instrument struck by the blow of some external force instead of a player's hand, they are not meaningless; they are not absurd; they do not imply that one portion of our ideas is asleep, while another is beginning to wake. On the contrary, they are psychical phenomena of complete validity.

—SIGMUND FREUD

Personal opinions are more or less arbitrary judgments and may be all wrong. We are never sure of being right; therefore we should seek the facts provided by dreams. Dreams are objective facts. They do not answer our expectations.

—CARL G. JUNG

Give me poison to die or dreams to live.

—GUNNAR EKELOF

It may be those who do most, dream most.

—STEPHEN LEACOCK

A man may dream both good and bad dreams in one and the same night. Nay more, in the self-same dream he may see both good and bad things, which the interpreter must separate in judgment.

—ARTIMEDORUS

Dreams are the touchstones of our character.

—HENRY DAVID THOREAU

The best interpreter of dreams is the man who can best grasp similarities, i.e., who is a master of metaphor, which is "the one thing that cannot be learnt from others."

—ARISTOTLE

Whoso regardeth dreams is like him that catcheth at a shadow and followeth after the wind.

—APOCRYPHA, Ecclesiastes 34:2

It is *never* "only a dream," John Constantine.

—NEIL GAIMAN

A motion picture is a dream. When you see it you are in the dark. A movie involves drawing on your unconscious in the same way that dreams come out of the unconscious.

—MIKE NICHOLS

How or why had I been shown an unreleased roll of my life film?

—RUDYARD KIPLING

I was not looking for my dreams to interpret my life but rather for my life to interpret my dreams.

—SUSAN SONTAG

Reality can destroy the dream, why shouldn't the dream destroy reality?

—GEORGE MOORE

What we experience in dreams, so long as we experience it frequently, is in the end just as much a part of the total economy of our soul as anything we "really" experience.

—FRIEDRICH NIETZSCHE

The blank page gives the right to dream.

—GASTON BACHELARD

In our dreams—I know it!—we *do* make the journeys we seem to make, we *do* see the people we seem to see, the people, the horses, the cats.

—MARK TWAIN

Dreams are nothing but incoherent ideas, occasioned by partial or imperfect sleep.

—BENJAMIN RUSH

The eye sees a thing more clearly in dreams than the imagination awake.

—LEONARDO DA VINCI

Looking at the stars always makes me dream. I dream my paintings then I paint my dreams.

—VINCENT VAN GOGH

But sure there is need of other remedies other than dreaming, a weak contention of art against nature.

—MICHEL DE MONTAIGNE

Seek art and abstraction in nature by dreaming in the presence of it.

—PAUL GAUGIN

As one, who from a dream awakened, straight. All he hath seen, forgets; yet still retains impressions of the feeling in his dream.

—DANTE ALIGHIERI

...the true state of creative genius is allied to reverie, or dreaming.

—OLIVER WENDELL HOLMES

Hope is a waking dream.

—ARISTOTLE

Was it a vision, or a waking dream?
Fled is that music: do I wake or sleep?

—JOHN KEATS

I do not know whether I was then a man dreaming I was a butterfly or whether I am now a butterfly dreaming I am a man.

—Chuang Tse

Beautiful dreamer, wake unto me
Starlight and dewdrop are waiting for thee.

—Stephen Foster

The rules of dreaming are not general, and therefore cannot satisfy all persons, they admit of various interpretations

—Artimedorus

We are
in a time so strange
that living equals dreaming
and this teaches me
That man
dreams his life awake.

—PEDRO CALDERON DE LA BARCA

In a word, as we often dream that we dream and heap vision upon vision, it may well be that this life itself is but a dream...from which we awake at death.

—BLAISE PASCAL

All that we see or seem
Is but a dream within a dream.

—EDGAR ALLAN POE

Those who dream by day are cognizant of many things which escape those who dream only by night.

—Edgar Allan Poe

All men dream, but not equally. Those who dream by night in the dusty recesses of their minds wake in the day to find that it was vanity; but the dreamers of the day are dangerous men, for they may act their dream with open eyes to make it possible.

—T. E. Lawrence

There is nothing like dreams to create the future. Utopia today, flesh and blood tomorrow.

—Victor Hugo

The world dreams of things to come, and then in due season arouses itself to their realization.

—Alfred North Whitehead

If a little dreaming is dangerous, the cure for it is not to dream less, but to dream more, to dream all the time.

—Marcel Proust

Maybe the wildest dreams are merely the needful preludes to the truth.

—Alfred, Lord Tennyson

Nothing happens unless first a dream.

—Carl Sandburg

What is now proved was once only imagin'd.

—WILLIAM BLAKE

If you don't have a dream, how are you going to make a dream come true?

—OSCAR HAMMERSTEIN

Dream no small dreams for they have no power to move the hearts of men.

—JOHANN WOLFGANG VON GOETHE

To dream the impossible dream.

—JOE DARION

In dreams and in love, there are no impossibilities.

—JANOS ARANY, poet

I like the dreams of the future better than the history of the past.

—THOMAS JEFFERSON

In dreams begin responsibilities.

—DELMORE SCHWARTZ

Dreams pass into the reality of action. From action stems the dream again; and this interdependence produces the highest form of living.

—ANAIS NIN

In a dream you are never eighty.

—ANNE SEXTON

Common sense tells us that the things of the
earth exist only a little and that true reality is only
in dreams.

—CHARLES BAUDELAIRE

...in dreams we put on the likeness of that more
universal, truer, more eternal man dwelling in the
darkness of primordial night. There it is still the
whole, and the whole is in him, indistinguishable
from nature and bare from all egohood.

—CARL G. JUNG

They tease me now telling me it was only a dream. But does it matter whether it was a dream or reality if the dream made known to me the truth?

—FYDOR DOSTOEVSKY

…dreaming dreams no mortal ever dreamed before.

—EDGAR ALLAN POE

I don't use drugs, my dreams are frightening enough.

—M. C. ESCHER

All the things one has forgotten scream for help in dreams.

—ELIAS CANETTI

What we see at night are the unhappy relics that
    we neglected while awake.
The dream is often the revenge of things
    scorned or the reproach of beings deserted.

—ANATOLE FRANCE

What happens to a dream deferred?
Does it dry up
Like a raisin in the sun?
Or does it explode?

—LANGSTON HUGHES

The enormous tragedy of the dream in the peasant's
bent shoulders.

—EZRA POUND

Of old the world on dreaming fed
Gray Truth is now her painted toy.

—WILLIAM BUTLER YEATS

The dream of reason produces monsters.

—FRANCISCO JOSE DE GOYA Y LUCIENTES

History is a nightmare from which I'm trying to awake.

—JAMES JOYCE

Now o'er the one-half world
Nature seems dead, and wicked dreams abuse
The curtained sleep.

—WILLIAM SHAKESPEARE

There's no time to lose, I heard her say
Catch your dreams before they slip away.

—MICK JAGGER/KEITH RICHARDS

Either we have no dreams or we have interesting ones. We need to learn to be awake in the same way, either not at all or in an interesting way.

—FRIEDRICH NIETZSCHE

Dreams may contain ineluctable truths, philosoph-ical pronouncements, illusions, wild fantasies, memories, plans, anticipations, irrational experi-ences, even telepathic visions and heaven knows what besides.

—CARL G. JUNG

...the dream (then) represents the largest visible circuit or 'the outermost envelope' of all the circuits.

—GILLES DELEUZE

I wake up in the morning with a dream in my eyes.

—ALLEN GINSBERG

...the fact that everybody in the world dreams every night ties all mankind together shall we say in one unspoken Union and also proves that the world is really transcendental.

—JACK KEROUAC

There couldn't be a society of people who didn't dream. They'd be dead in two weeks.

—WILLIAM S. BURROUGHS

The soul in sleep gives proof of its divine nature.

—Cicero

What if you slept
And what if
In your sleep
You dreamed
And what if
In your dream
You went to heaven
And there plucked a strange and beautiful flower
And what if
When you awoke
You had that flower in your hand
Ah, what then?

—Samuel Taylor Coleridge

Sleep hath its own world
And a wide reality
And dreams in that development have breath
and Tears
and tortures and the touch of joy.

—George Gordon, Lord Byron

To sleep, perchance to dream, Ay, there's the rub
For in that sleep of death what dreams may come.

—William Shakespeare

The world is seldom what it seems; to man, who
dimly sees, realities appear as dreams, and dreams
realities.

—Samuel Johnson

The net of the sleeper catches fish.

—GREEK PROVERB

Even sleepers are workers and collaborators in what goes on in the Universe.

—HERACLITUS

Every one that sleeps is beautiful...every thing in the dim night is beautiful

—WALT WHITMAN

Redeem
The unread vision in the higher dream.

—T. S. ELIOT

Dreams are today's answers to tomorrow's questions.

—EDGAR CAYCE

And there are two states for that person, the one here in this world, the other in the other world, and as a third, an intermediate state, the state of sleep, when, in that intermediate state, he sees both these states together.

—BRIHADARMAYAKA UPANISHAD

Your old men shall dream dreams, your young men shall see visions.

—THE BIBLE, Joel 2:28

In a dream, in a vision of the night, when deep sleep falleth upon men, in slumberings upon the bed; then he openeth the ears of men and sealeth their instructions.

—THE BIBLE, Job 33:15

It is most important to unite
Dream yoga with illusory body
And practice them in day time and night.

—MILAREPA

I have spread my dreams under your feet
Tread softly because you tread on my dreams.

—W. B. YEATS

Two-gates the silent house of Sleep adorn
Of polished ivory this, that of transparent horn:
True visions through transparent horn arise
Thro' polished ivory pass deluding lies.

—Virgil, *The Aeneid*

Friend, many and many a dream is mere confusion,
a cobweb of no consequence at all.
Two gates for ghostly dreams there are: one gateway
of honest horn, and one of ivory,
issuing by the ivory gate are dreams
of glittering illusion, fantasies,
but those that come through solid polished horn
may be born out, if mortals only knew them.

—Homer, *The Odyssey*

Our dreams are a second life. I have ever been able to penetrate without a shudder those ivory and horned gates that separate us from the invisible world.

—GERARD DE NERVAL

deeds cannot dream what dreams can do

—E.E. CUMMINGS

There have been times when I have fallen asleep in tears but in my dreams the most charming forms have come to cheer me up and I have risen fresh and joyful.

—JOHANN WOLFGANG VON GOETHE

Keep true to the dreams of thy youth.

—JOHANN VON SCHILLER

Learn from your dreams what you lack.

—W. H. AUDEN

You may say that I'm a dreamer but I'm not the only one.

—JOHN LENNON

In dreams, I walk with you
In dreams, I talk with you
In dreams you're mine
All of the time.

—ROY ORBISON

A dream is a scripture and many scriptures are nothing but dreams.

—UMBERTO ECO

To dream is to sleep with illustrations in the text.

—EUGENIO D'ORS Y ROVIRA

Dreams, books, are each a world; and books, we know, are a substantial world.

—WILLIAM WORDSWORTH

If you wish to form a clear judgment on your friends, consult your dreams.

—KARL KRAUS

What we do in our dreams we also do when we are awake: we invent and make up the person we are dealing with—and immediately forget that we have done it.

—FRIEDRICH NIETZSCHE

The dreams of mankind are the material of all the beautiful and good things it has made.

—BERNARD MOITESSIER

In bed my real love has always been the sleep that rescued me by allowing me to dream.

—LUIGI PIRANDELLO

Anyone can escape into sleep, we are all geniuses when we dream.

—E. M. CIORAN

We are afloat
On our dreams as on a barge made of ice
Shot through with questions and fissures
    of starlight.

—JOHN ASHBERY

One of the characteristics of the dream is that nothing surprises us in it. With no regret, we agree to live in it with strangers, completely cut off from our habits and friends.

—JEAN COCTEAU

Oh, life could be a dream (sh-boom)
If I could take you up in paradise above (sh-boom)
If you would tell me I'm the only one you love.

—popularized by the THE CREW CUTS

The greatest achievement was at first and for a time, a dream, the oak sleeps in the acorn, the bird awaits in the egg, and in the highest vision of the soul, a waking angel stirs.

—WILLIAM JAMES

Dreaming, after all, is a form of planning.

—GLORIA STEINEM

Dreams, aspirations of presence!

—TED BERRIGAN

I dreamed I saw Joe Hill last night
Alive as you or me
Says I "But Joe you're ten years dead"
I never died, says he
I never died, says he.

—EARLY AMERICAN UNION SONG

Ideologies separate us. Dreams and anguish bring us together.

—EUGENE IONESCO

What dreaming does is give us the fluidity to enter into other worlds by destroying our sense of knowing this world.

—CARLOS CASTENADA

The dream is the best proof that we are not as firmly locked up in our skins as it would seem.

—FRIEDRICH HEBBEL

Dreaming permits each and every one of us to be quietly and safely insane every night of our lives.

—WILLIAM C. DEMENT

The value of lucid dreams is that you can have any imagined experience without consequence.

—STEVEN LA BERGE

Sometimes while asleep, a man may judge what he sees is a dream, discerning as it were between things and images.

—THOMAS AQUINAS

The personality is the same in dreaming life as in waking life.

—ALFRED ADLER

I have always been amazed at the way an ordinary observer lends so much more credence and attaches so much more importance to waking events than to those occurring in dreams. Man is above all the plaything of his memory.

—ANDRE BRETON

Dreams don't lie but liars dream.

—Milton Kramer

I believe in the future resolution of these two states, dream and reality, which are apparently so contradictory, into a sort of absolute reality, a *surreality*, so to speak.

—Andre Breton

I divide my time as follows: half the time I sleep, the other half I dream. I never dream when I sleep, for that would be a pity, for sleeping is the highest accomplishment of genius.

—Søren Kierkegaard

An artist is a dreamer consenting to dream of the actual world.

—GEORGE SANTAYANA

If someone were to tell me I had twenty years left, and ask me how I'd like to spend them, I'd reply "Give me two hours a day of activity, and I'll take the other twenty two in dreams."

—LUIS BUNUEL

Dreams, dreams, dreams, the domain of dreams widens at each step. Dreams, dreams dreams, the blue sun of dreams drives the steel-eyed beasts back to their lairs at last.

—LOUIS ARAGON

Dream as though you'll live forever; live as though you'll die today.

—JAMES DEAN

Life is more fantastic than our dreams.

—RIDLEY SCOTT

Do Androids Dream of Electric Sheep?

—PHILIP K. DICK

Dreams are the subtle Dowser
That make us rich an Hour
Then fling us poor
Out of the purple door.

—EMILY DICKINSON

Dreams are the bright creatures of power and legend who sport on earth in the night season and melt away with the first beams of the sun.

—CHARLES DICKENS

I've dreamt in my life dreams that have stayed with me ever after, and changed my ideas; they've gone through and through me like wine through water, and altered the color of my mind.

—EMILY BRONTE

Dreams have only the pigmentation of fact.

—DJUNA BARNES

Here we are all by day; by night we are hurled
By dreams, each one into a several world.

—ROBERT HERRICK

We live, as we dream...alone.

—JOSEPH CONRAD

The dream is an existential message...it is the message of yourself to yourself. Every part, every situation in the dream...every aspect of it is a part of the dreamer, but a part that is to some extent, disowned.

—FRITZ PERLS

What if nothing exists and we're all in somebody's dream? or what's worse, what if only that fat guy in the third row exists?

—WOODY ALLEN

If there were dreams to sell,
Merry and sad to tell
And the crier rung his bell.
What would you buy?

—THOMAS LOVELL BEDDOES, "Dream Pedlar"

My biggest nightmare is I'm driving home and get sick and go to the hospital. I say: 'Please help me.' And the people say: 'Hey you look like…' And I'm dying while they're wondering whether I am Barbra Streisand.

—BARBRA STREISAND

…confusion and
Dismay, the usual consequence of dreams.

—GEORGE GORDON, LORD BYRON

I have had dreams and I have had nightmares. I overcame my nightmares because of my dreams.

—JONAS SALK

In sleep the doors of the mind are shut and thoughts come jumping in at the windows.

—JAMES BOSWELL

Now o'er the one half world
Nature seems dead, and wicked dreams abuse
The curtained sleep.

—WILLIAM SHAKESPEARE

Sweet dreams, form a shade o'er my lovely
    infant's head
Sweet dreams of pleasant streams
By happy, silent, moony beams.

—WILLIAM BLAKE

Sweet dreams till sunbeams find you
Sweet dreams that leave all worries behind you
But in your dreams whatever they be
Dream a little dream of me.

—GUS KAHN

You see things, and you say "Why?" But I dream things that never were, and I say "Why not?"

—GEORGE BERNARD SHAW

Now, I say to you today my friends, even though we face the difficulties of today and tomorrow, I still have a dream.

—MARTIN LUTHER KING, JR.

Revolution only needs good dreamers who remember their dreams.

—Tennessee Williams

So flowerlike is (the dream) in its candor and veracity that it makes is blush for the deceitfulness of our lives.

—Carl G. Jung

Some people sleep so well because their dreams are so boring.

—Germaine de Stael

They are not long, the days of wine and roses,
Out of a misty dream
Our path merges a while, then closes.

—Ernest Dowson

A man is not old until regrets take the place of dreams.

—JOHN BARRYMORE

People who insist on telling their dreams are among the terrors of the breakfast table.

—MAX BEERBOHM

It has never been my object to record my dreams, just the determination to realize them.

—MAN RAY

We do not feel as if we were producing the dreams, it is rather as if the dreams came to us. They are not subject to our control but obey their own laws. They are obviously autonomous psychic complexes which form themselves out of their own material.

—CARL G. JUNG

Some say dreams are poetry. Some say that dreaming is an art. I say dreams are the eyes of the mind. These eyes start to see when we switch off the light.

—GENEVIEVE BOURIS

I am amazed that we don't have to pay for viewing our dreams. They are, after all, a kind of television for sleepers.

—ALBERTO SORDI

The imprint a dream leaves is no less real than that left by a foot.

—GEORGES DUBY

Reverie is not a mind vacuum. It is rather the gift of an hour which knows the plenitude of the soul.

—GASTON BACHALARD

The reveries of the true and simple are prophetic.

—RALPH WALDO EMERSON

Every night I hope and pray a dream lover will come my way.

—BOBBY DARIN

Surrealism rests on the belief in the superior reality of hitherto neglected associations, in the omnipotence of dreams, in the disinterested play of thought...

—ANDRE BRETON

Objects seen in dreams should be manufactured and put on sale.

—ANDRE BRETON

People do not dream, they are dreamt. We undergo our dreams.

—CARL G. JUNG

I'll let you be in my dream, if I can be in yours.

—BOB DYLAN

In the process of dreams, man expresses real life.

—FRIEDRICH NIETZSCHE

While you are in a dream, it is reality, and the bear-bite hurts; hurts in a perfectly real way.

—MARK TWAIN

We are such stuff
as dreams are made on, and our little Life
is rounded with sleep.

—WILLIAM SHAKESPEARE

Is the jailer envious of his prisoner's dreams?

—GERARD DE NERVAL

When I sleep I sleep and do not dream because it is as well that I am what I seem when I am in my bed and dream.

—GERTRUDE STEIN

It is one of the blessings of this world that few people see visions and dream dreams.

—ZORA NEALE HURSTON

We all dream; we do not understand our dreams, yet we act as if nothing strange goes on in our sleep minds, strange at least by comparison with the logical, purposeful doings of our minds when we are awake.

—ERICH FROMM

Whenever I want you, all I have to do, is
Dream, dream dream dream.

—EVERLY BROTHERS

Our dreams are firsthand creations, rather than residues of waking life.

—JACKIE GLEASON

Not all lucid dreams are useful but they all have a sense of wonder about them. If you must sleep through a third of your life, why should you sleep through your dreams, too?

—STEPHEN LABERGE

Dreams are the wanderings of the spirit though all nine heavens and all nine earths.

—LU YEN

All that we see or seem
Is but a dream within a dream.

—EDGAR ALLEN POE

Where all is but dream, reasoning and arguments
are of no use, truth and knowledge nothing.

—JOHN LOCKE

My sleep is made cold
By a recurrent dream…

—PHILIP LARKIN

What is life? A madness. What is life? An illusion,
a shadow, a story. And the greatest good is little
enough; for all life is a dream, and dreams themselves are only dreams.

—PEDRO CALDERÓN DE LA BARCA

They who dream by day are cognizant of many things which escape those who dream only by night.

—Edgar Allan Poe

I believe that dreams—daydreams, you know, with your eyes wide open and your brain machinery whizzing—are likely to lead to the betterment

—L. Frank Baum

Our truest life is when we are in dreams awake.

—Henry David Thoreau

Give them pleasure—the same pleasure they have when they wake up from a nightmare.

—Alfred Hitchcock

How many of our daydreams would darken into nightmares, were there a danger of their coming true!

—LOGAN PEARSALL SMITH

In my hungry fatigue, and shopping for images,
I went into the neon fruit supermarket,
    dreaming of your enumerations!

—ALLEN GINSBERG

If I had been told of them when waking, I should not have been able to acknowledge them as parts of my past experience. But placed as they were before me, in dreams like intuitions, and clothed in all their evanescent circumstances and accompanying feelings, I *recognized* them instantaneously.

—THOMAS DE QUINCEY

I have dreamed of the green night of the dazzled
    snows,
the kiss rising slowly to the eyes of the seas,
the circulation of undreamed-of saps,
and the yellow-blue awakenings of singing
    phosphorus!

—Arthur Rimbaud

Sleep shall repeat the echoes of the day to another
and unfatigued inner sense of dreams, and awak-
ing shall bear repetition of birth into newer and
still more enchanting life.

—Fitz Hugh Ludlow

It is in our idleness, in our dreams, that the sub-
merged truth sometimes comes to the top.

—Virginia Woolf

When I'm in the middle of a dream
Stay in bed, float up stream
Please, don't wake me, no, don't shake me
Leave me where I am—I'm only sleeping

—LENNON AND MCCARTNEY

Life is at best a dream and at worst a nightmare from which you cannot escape.

—MARK TWAIN

We'll just be dreaming of animation night and day.

—PATTI SMITH

Ernest, don't talk about action. It is the last resource of those who know not how to dream.

—OSCAR WILDE

her babies can dream
but dreams begin like the end
shot into eternity

        —ALLEN GINSBERG AND THE CLASH

The end of wisdom is to dream high enough to lose the dream in the seeking of it.

        —WILLIAM FAULKNER

I dream a lot. I do more painting when I'm not painting. It's in the subconscious.

        —ANDREW WYETH

While armchair travelers dream of going places, traveling armchairs dream of staying put.

        —ANN TYLER

Love is an attempt to change a piece of a dream world into reality.

—THEODOR REIK

Dream research is a wonderful field. All you do is sleep for a living.

—STEPHEN LaBERGE

The question will remain, where does the dream end for me?

—MARIO CUOMO

I've lived to bury my desires,
And see my dreams corrode with rust

—ALEXANDER PUSHKIN

Desolate dreams pursue me out of sleep;
Weeping I wake; waking, I weep, I weep.

—EDNA ST. VINCENT MILLAY

Each dream finds at last its form; there is a drink for every thirst, and love for every heart.

—GUSTAVE FLAUBERT

Man no longer dreams over a book in which a soft voice, a constant companion, observes, exhorts, or sighs with him through the pangs of youth and age. Today he is more likely to sit before a screen and dream the mass dream which comes from outside.

—LOREN EISELEY

I do what many dream of, all their lives,

—Robert Browning

Perhaps life is just that...a dream and a fear.

—Joseph Conrad

You shoot me in a dream, you better wake up and apologize.

—Quentin Tarrantino

But really a novel goes as dreams go in sleeping at night and some dreams are like anything and some dreams are like something and some dreams change and some dreams are quiet and some dreams are not. And some dreams are just what any one would do only a little different always just a little different and that is what a novel is.

—GERTRUDE STEIN

He hath awakened from the dream of life.

—PERCY BYSSHE SHELLEY

Fathoms down, fathoms down, how I'll dream fast asleep.

—HERMAN MELVILLE

"I don't like belonging to another person's dream," she went on in a rather complaining tone: "I've a great mind to go and wake him, and see what happens!"

—LEWIS CARROLL

I was by degrees awakened as from a dream, and feared that my whole life could properly be counted nothing else but a fantastic vision.

—SARAH FIELDING

Eyes I dare not meet in dreams
In death's dream kingdom
These do not appear.

—T. S. ELIOT

A man that is born falls into a dream like a man who falls into the sea. If he tries to climb out into the air as inexperienced people endeavour to do, he drowns.

—Joseph Conrad

Perhaps it is nothingness which is real and our dream which is non-existent, but then we feel that these musical phrases, and the notions related to the dream, are nothing too.

—Marcel Proust

Every concrete object
has abstract value, is timeless
in the dream parallel.

—Hilda Doolittle

We are things of dry hours and the involuntary plan,
Grayed in, and gray. "Dream" makes a giddy
    sound, not strong
Like "rent," "feeding a wife," "satisfying a man."

—GWENDOLYN BROOKS

I'm inexcusably happy. Something magical has happened to me, like a dream, when you're frightened, panic-stricken, and all of a sudden you wake up and all the horrors are no more. I have waked up.

—LEO TOLSTOY

Its things are borrowed, and it will take the loan from the borrower: and it is like the confused visions of the sleeper, and the dream of the dreamer, as though it were the sarab [mirage] of the plain, which the thirsty imagineth to be water: the Devil adorneth it for man until death.

—Stories from THOUSAND AND ONE NIGHTS

Does Britannia, when it sleeps, dream? Is America her dream?

—Thomas Pynchon

They tell this tale of its foundation: men of various nations had an identical dream. They saw a woman running at night through an unknown city; she was seen from behind, with long hair and she was naked. They dreamed of pursuing her. As they twisted and turned, each of them lost her. After the dream they set out in search of that city; they never found it, but they found one another; they decided to build a city like the one in the dream.

—Italo Calvino

This life we live is a strange dream, and I don't believe at all any account men give of it.

—Henry David Thoreau

Sanity is a madness put to good uses; waking life is a dream controlled.

—George Santayana

We sometimes congratulate ourselves at the moment of waking from a troubled dream; it may be so the moment after death.

—Nathaniel Hawthorne

Like man and wife who nightly keep
Inconsequent debate in sleep
As they dream side by side.

—Robert Graves

(sleep wake hope and then) they
said their nevers they slept their dream

—E.E. CUMMINGS

When you're alone in the middle of the night and
    you wake in a sweat and a hell of a fright
When you're alone in the middle of the bed and
    you wake like someone hit you in the head
You've had a cream of a nightmare dream and
    you've got the hoo-ha's coming to you.

—T. S. ELIOT

I dream about that sometimes—and wake up
screaming.

—PHILIP LARKEN

The only limits are, as always, those of vision.

—JAMES BROUGHTON

The best way to make your dreams comes true is to wake up.

—PAUL VALERY